The Bible is Black History

PERSONAL WORKBOOK

Dr. Theron D. Williams

TABLE OF CONTENTS

PREFACE

Since the release of *The Bible is Black History*, I have been on a national tour promoting it by conducting workshops and lecture series. Whether the setting is in a church, college or university campus, religious convention, or with small groups, there is never enough time to exhaust all of the important themes contained in the book. Thus far, I have been invited to return to every venue for a second lecture or workshop series. One might think it flattering to receive a return invitation from the host before one leaves the venue, but the re-invitations only verify my suspicion that I left my audiences with more questions than answers.

For the most part, my audiences seem to have been aware that Black people comprised the Old and New Testament communities and that they somehow share a special, intimate connection with those communities. Some of them had heard it mentioned in sermons by their pastors, some had read books or articles that hinted at this notion while others felt an intuitive connection to the people of the Bible beyond a spiritual one.

Nevertheless, they had no empirical evidence to prove it. *The Bible is Black History* seeks to provide the academic and scientific veracity my audiences need to substantiate their inclination that their connection to the biblical congregation of Israel is not just spiritual through their acceptance of Christ as Savior, but a genetic, hereditary, and consanguineous connection.

The information contained in *The Bible is Black History* is empowering to my audiences, which are mostly comprised of African-Americans. For their entire lives, they have been taught that their ancestors played no role in salvation history; that Black people were relegated to the sidelines of history while White people won salvation for the world. The European Jews, who now occupy Israel, were esteemed by most Black people as the descendants of the biblical Israelites. For generations, Black people have accepted the lie that all of the biblical heroes were White. Throughout most of the African-American existence, it has been common practice for them to bedeck the walls of their homes, churches, schools, and businesses with pictures of White Jesus and other White biblical heroes. It is refreshing and liberating to most African-Americans to have proof that Black people were the authors and champions of salvation history; and that when God decided to visit planet Earth, God did so using the black body of Jesus from Nazareth.

In every workshop I am asked, "Since the Bible is a book about faith, why should the skin color of the biblical character matter?" The response to this question is twofold. First, the truth must always matter. And secondly, the critical question is, if skin color shouldn't matter, why has there been an intentional campaign to color the characters of the Bible White from Black? These are the questions that *The Bible is Black History* examines.

The Bible is Black History Personal Workbook is designed for personal or small group study. It intends to draw the reader into a dialogue, not only with the members of the small group, but also with the author on key themes of the book. It is my hope that after reading *The Bible is Black History,* along with the personal workbook, the student will come away from the study with more answers than questions.

INTRODUCTION

The introduction of *The Bible is Black History* explores the notion that because of global domination by the Western World, significant White historical figures are celebrated while others are largely ignored. However, there are historical personalities who are not of European descent like Jesus, Moses, apostle Paul, Queen Cleopatra, Queen Nefertiti, and others whose contributions to world civilization are undeniable and cannot be overlooked. In these cases, the historical figures are simply whitewashed. Even though Israel is located on the continent of Africa, the Israelites are not recognized as Africans by the dominant culture. It doesn't matter that DNA evidence proves that the father of modern humans originates in East Africa near Ethiopia, which corresponds with the biblical location of the Land of Eden; Adam and Eve are stubbornly depicted as White people in mainstream media.

The constant bombardment of these false biblical images, conjured up by this culture, has indelibly branded the world's consciousness.

Most of the world have embraced these images as truth, including people of color, no matter how psychologically and spiritually damaging they may be. *The Bible is Black History Institute* has taken on the task of promoting more valid biblical images that reflect the likeness of the people who wrote the Bible. The likes of Dr. Cain Hope Felder in his book, *Troubling Biblical Waters*; and William Dwight McKissic's book, *Beyond Roots: In Search of Blacks in the Bible*; Walter Arthur McCray's work, *The Black Presence in the* Bible and others, have already made monumental contributions in the effort of reconditioning the Black community's consciousness to bring it into the knowledge of the truth about biblical depictions. It is my hope that the accumulative effect of the works of these and other scholars would someday be weighty enough to move the African-American community, at-large, to at least begin to consider the possibility that their ancestors played a significant role in salvation history, and that the mainstream depictions of the biblical champions are entirely false.

Study Questions

1. Can you prove on which continent Israel is located?

2. What is the probable location of the Land of Eden? How can you prove it?

3. What are your thoughts about the so-called Middle East? On which continent is it located? What countries make up the so-called Middle East? When did this area become known as the Middle East and why?

4. Why do you think the ancient Egyptians, Ethiopians, and Hebrews are depicted as White people in Western culture?

5. Why do you think the biblical writers rarely used skin color to describe the biblical characters?

6. What is the difference between vitiligo and Hansen's disease?

7. When the Bible describes someone as being leprous, are the symptoms more akin to vitiligo or Hansen's disease?

8. How does Lamentations 4:7-9 prove that the princes of Israel were not White men?

CHAPTER ONE

IN THE BEGINNING

Most people agree that the human race has a common father and mother. Dr. Spencer Wells led the Genographic Project to discover the who, when and where of the origin of modern humanity. His research concluded that the father of modern humans is a Black man from Africa that dates back more than 60,000 years. The Bible identifies him as Adam. Dr. Wells' team created a bust that depicts the facial features of the father of modern humans. (See page 31 in The Bible is Black History).

The concept of the Imago Dei explores the idea that God endows humans with unique qualities that make them like God and unlike the creatures in the animal kingdom. Theologians have argued for centuries what these divine qualities could be. Conceptions about the Imago Dei is expansive, including the notion of human intelligence; human capacity to choose moral living; God's activity of imparting God's self in humanity when God "breathed into his nostrils the breath of life"; which God did not do for the animal

1

kingdom and countless suggestions. A re-examination of Genesis 1:26-27 indicates the word 'image' implies that God created humans to look like God physically.

Study Questions

1. How is it that the father of modern humans (Adam) originates in Africa?

2. Other than the fact that Adam originates in Africa, what other evidence is there to prove Adam's race?

3. What is the Imago Dei and how must it be redefined?

4. Read the description of the location of the Land of Eden in Genesis 2:9-14. According to this passage, does Dr. Wells' findings concerning the place of origin of humankind contradict or confirm the Genesis passage, or does it fail to confirm or contradict it?

CHAPTER TWO

NOAH AND HIS OFFSPRING

Every event in the Genesis story from the Creation (Genesis 1:1) to Noah's construction of the Ark (Genesis 7) took place in Africa. After the Great Flood, the biblical story scene changes to Mt. Ararat, which is located on the border of Persia. This scene provides the backdrop for the repopulation of the earth through Noah's three sons Shem, Japheth, and Ham. A ton of misinformation is in circulation concerning Noah's offspring. Some argue that Noah's sons were born as three different races. Racist propaganda changed the meaning of Noah son's names. Ham's name means, "The father of a multitude" but racist biblicists manipulated its meaning to "Hot or Black." He is celebrated as the father of the Africans. According to racist puffery, Ham's punishment for looking on his drunken father's nakedness was to be turned Black. Accordingly, the meaning of Shem's name was also manipulated from its true meaning, "famous or renown" to "dusty or light brown." Supposedly, he is the progenitor of Asian races. Finally, Japheth,

Noah's middle son's name was corrupted from its original meaning, "That he may expand his boarders"; to "beautiful, white" and he is the father of the Europeans.

As we shall later learn in this study, these color designations were applied to Noah's offspring to justify the White Male Supremacy System's Hierarchy of Humanity. In this hierarchy, White people are at the top; inferior people of color are on the lower rung, with Black people at the very bottom. A casual reading of the story of Noah and his offspring, however, contradicts all of these racist notions that somehow seeped into the Sacred Text.

Study Questions

1. How and when did the biblical story move from Africa to Persia?

2. Why is Noah a key figure in the origin of the races?

3. Shem is Noah's oldest son. What does his name mean and why is it significant?

4. Japheth is Noah's middle son. Though neither he nor his offspring appear to be important in the biblical story, why is Japheth significant in human history?

5. Ham is Noah's youngest son. Why is he relevant in biblical and secular history?

6. Who is Canaan and why is he a central figure in the biblical story?

7. Who did Noah curse and why? What does the curse imply?

CHAPTER THREE

THE ISRAELITES' MIGRATIONS TO AFRICA

The biblical Hebrews experienced an extremely turbulent history in the land of Israel. From the time they conquered Canaan, as recorded in the Book of Joshua, until the Romans destroyed Israel in CE 70, this community faced one catastrophe after another. There were numerous volunteer migrations among the Hebrews and at least two forced deportations. Of all the migrations and deportations this community endured, there is no historical documentation that any were to Europe. There is however, historical and DNA evidence to prove that the Hebrews, were of African descent because they lived in Israel, which is in North East Africa, migrated further in the continent.

There has been much discussion about what became of the Lost Ten Tribes of Israel. Extra-biblical sources such as the apocryphal Book of Esdras may shed light on what could have become of at least a remnant of the Lost Tribes of Israel.

Study Questions

1. To where were the Hebrews deported and to where did they migrate?

2. Do you think the Lost Tribes of Israel could have migrated from Assyria to Igbo Land, Nigeria? Explain.

3. Do you think the legend of Menelik is probable? Explain.

4. Why do you think there are no biblical accounts and very sketchy historical reports of a Hebrew migration to Europe?

CHAPTER FOUR

JESUS CHRIST

J esus Christ is the most significant historical figure of all times. The spiritual, political, economic and social movement that our Lord initiated in the first century CE still influences the work of authentic ministry today. His vicarious death on the cross at Mt. Calvary still satisfies God's requirement for salvation and human-divine reconciliation. The resurrection of our Lord is the single most pivotal event in human history because it confirms the reality that God, indeed, incarnated God's Self in a Black man who lived in first century Israel in the peasant region of Galilee in a small village called Nazareth. His resurrection also verifies that Jesus is not just another influential teacher, preacher, or charismatic leader. He is more than just another faith healer or exorcist. His resurrection further proves that He is who He said He is and whom the earliest followers believed Him to be, the Christ, God's Messiah and Savior of the world.

We must not lose sight of the fact, however, that Jesus was a human being who had a fully human experience. He lived, loved, laughed, cried, became hungry and thirsty; experienced fatigue, frustration, loneliness, and embarrassment. He knew joy and sorrow, pleasure and pain. He even experienced death. He was fully human, meaning He was flesh and blood. He bore the indigenous physical characteristics of His race and was immersed in His ethnicity.

Being who He is, it is expected that communities worldwide would want to have consanguineous ties to Jesus. However, the Europeans have been the most successful at co-opting Jesus as a member of their race. The traditional Western images of Jesus represent the success the Europeans have enjoyed at making Jesus one of them. These images are the most replicated in human history. They are also the most recognized representation of Jesus of Nazareth. Despite the historical and archeological evidence that a man born in the first century African nation of Israel, and according the genealogy provided in the Gospel of Matthew 1:1-17; would not have looked anything like the traditional images. These images are propagated even more forcefully by people who know the truth.

The critical question is not what difference does His color make? But, more importantly, why does European culture insist on forcing these false images upon society when historical and DNA evidence do not substantiate its supposition? To make this question even more pressing is the fact that we know that these images are variations of Cesare Borgia.

Study Guide

1. Why is the historical Jesus so important?

2. Why do you think the Europeans have been the most successful at co-opting Jesus as a member of their race?

3. Is the traditional image of Jesus disturbing to you? Explain.

4. Who is Cesare Borgia and why is he an essential figure in the Western depiction of Jesus?

5. Do you think Richard Neave's bust of a first century, thirty-something-year-old Hebrew man comes close to the image of Jesus? Explain.

6. Discuss Flavius Josephus' physical description of Jesus.

CHAPTER FIVE

THE APOSTLE PAUL AND THE EARLY CHURCH

Next to Jesus, apostle Paul is the most crucial figure in church history. No one but God could have chosen Paul to become the second most influential personality in Christendom after Jesus, Himself.

There are very few, if any, parallels between Pauline theology and *Jesusian theology* (the theology of Jesus). One's experience is the core of any authentic theological position. What is theology but one's interpretation of how God is at work in the world as one experiences the world? People who experience the world in similar ways tend to have analogous theological views as opposed to people who experience the world differently. For example, thinkers like Dr. James Cone, Dr. John Kinney, Dr. Fredrick Haynes, Dr. Martin Luther King, Jr. and others, who experience the world similarly, are likely to find theological common ground. Likewise, clergymen like Dr. Robert Jeffress, Dr. John Hagee, Rev. Franklin

Graham, and Dr. Billy Graham, who have common world experiences, are likely to have shared theological sentiments.

Jesus and the original twelve disciples' life experiences were far different from Paul's. Jesus and the Twelve, from their earliest childhoods lived their entire lives under the crushing colonial oppression of the Roman Empire. Jesus' life experiences informed His theology, shaped His message and dictated His ministry. Jesus' ministry was born out of a response to the injustices that disproportionately affected His community. Jesus and His earliest followers suffered want of life's basic needs due, in part to Rome's draconian economic policies and the ruthlessness with which those policies were enforced. The constant police presence in Galilee provided the colonial intimidation required to keep the conquered class *in their place*. Jesus' theology emerged from such a context.

Paul, on the other hand, knew nothing of colonial oppression. He was born a Roman citizen in the posh, European city of Tarsus. He was privileged, well educated, and often invoked his favor as a Roman citizen when he needed an advantage. As a Pharisee, he would have been among the Jewish elite class. As such, his lucrative lifestyle would have come at the exploitation of the peasant class of which Jesus and His disciples were a part. However, Paul's encounter with Christ on the Damascus Road would change his life forever. He would respond to Christ's call to preach the gospel to the Gentiles, which became his new vocation. Like other theologians, Paul's theology would have been greatly influenced by his experiences. Since Paul never experienced colonial oppression, exploitation or abject poverty because he was a member of the ruling class, he could not be expected to have a theology born out of those experiences.

Paul relied on the revelation of the Lord Jesus Christ, his background as an academician and Old Testament scholar to construct a theological position concerning what God was doing through Jesus Christ. Unlike Jesus, however, Paul was not so much concerned about social justice, as he was about preparing the church for the Second Coming of the Lord Jesus Christ. He preached the gospel so that people might be saved, saved in the sense that when Christ returns, they would be spared of His judgment. It is not that Paul was unaware of the Social injustices, though obvious as they were; his theological position however, was that when Christ returns (which he expected during his lifetime), He, Himself, would bring judgment to all injustice. Thus, Paul understood his calling to prepare the church for the End of the Age.

Although Paul's writings should be appreciated against the backdrop of Paul's eschatological beliefs, his writings serve as the perfect sequel to the earthly ministry of Jesus. Through the power of the Holy Spirit, Jesusian theology and Pauline theology are fused together in a cohesive, dynamic bond that empowers the church to change the world.

Paul is credited with taking the gospel to Europe. Some people argue in futility that White people gave the Africans Christianity when the truth is Paul, a Black man, was the one who introduced the gospel to the Europeans.

Study Questions

1. Why is apostle Paul an essential figure in church history?

2. How was Paul different from Jesus' original twelve disciples?

3. Why do you think the early Christians distrusted Paul?

4. What are your thoughts about the Great Commission in Matthew 28:18-20?

5. How can we comfortably assume that Paul was a Black man?

6. What do the images in the catacombs prove about the biblical heroes?

7. Take some time and examine your theology. Does your theology emerge from how you experience the world or have you embraced someone else's theological position from a different experience?

CHAPTER SIX

THE WHITEWASHING OF BIBLICAL HEBREW HISTORY

There has been a long and sustained effort to paint the entire Bible white from black. The European Jews, who occupy the land of Israel en masse today, have been accepted by many as the descendants of the biblical Hebrews. Thus, the terms Hebrew, Jew, and Israelite refer to the current occupants of Israel. In fact, the world, by and large, is convinced that the term Israeli is the modern translation for the term Israelite. Even though there is no credible historical evidence to prove that the European Jews have ever occupied Israel en masse before the 1930s doesn't seem to matter. They insist that they are the descendants of Father Abraham of the Bible.

The erroneous notion that the European Jews of today's Israel are the descendants of the biblical Jews has sparked an aggressive repatriation to Israel. This effort is mainly funded and supported by evangelical organizations.

There has never been a mass migration or deportation of the Hebrews to anywhere in Europe or Russia; therefore, when the Bible references the Jewish repatriation, it never mentions the Jews would return from anywhere in Europe. Isaiah 11:10-12, however, mentions Ethiopia, Lower Egypt and Upper Egypt and distant coastal lands. (Probably referring to Igbo Nigeria, which is on the west coast of Africa and the Chesapeake areas of Virginia and Maryland. These are the coastal lands to where the Hebrews were deported during the American slavery trade. See page 57 in The Bible is Black History), as places from which the Jews would repatriate Israel. Ironically, the Israeli government has deported many Ethiopian Jews and will not allow many of them entry. But the European Jews, who are not mentioned in the Bible among those Jews who would return, are welcomed into Israel with opened arms.

Study Guide

1. Discuss the differences between the Hebrews, Jews, Israelis, Semite, and Israelites?

2. When did Israel become an official state and why?

3. Who occupied Israel before the migration of the European Jews?

4. Why did the European Jews leave their European ancestral home to migrate to Israel?

5. According to Isaiah 11:10-12, from what nations will the Jews return to Israel?

6. Of all the great religious texts of the world, why do you think the Bible is the only one that does not depict its heroes in the image of the people who wrote it?

7. Do you think the Bible and the Christian faith were whitewashed? If so, how? If not, explain.

8. Did the Europeans steal the identity of the biblical Hebrews? If so, how did they accomplish it? If not, explain.

9. What does "Constantinian Christianity" mean?

10. Do you think the White Male Supremacy System manipulated the image of Jesus, His message, the Bible, and the church to advance its causes? If so, how?

11. Discuss how racism may have influenced the translation of Song of Songs 1:5.

12. Why is White Jesus so crucial in the advancement of the White Male Supremacy agenda?

13. How do African-Americans, and sometimes the Black church, participate in the perpetuation of the image of White Jesus? Discuss how this impacts the African-American community.

CHAPTER SEVEN

THE BIBLE IS BLACK HISTORY

The Bible is the story of a people of African descent who love their God and desire to follow His will for their community, but continually fail to live up to God's expectations. Their God is known by them not only for His power and justice, but also for His love, patience, mercy, and longsuffering. While repeatedly committing transgressions and idolatry, resulting in divine punishment, God is determined to accomplish His purpose on the earth through this community.

Study Questions

1. Discuss how the Bible is Black history

2. Why is it important for African-American youth to understand that the Bible is Black history?

3. Has the Black community been damaged by the way history is taught in most school systems?

CHAPTER EIGHT

THE CURRENT STRUGGLE OF THE BLACK CHURCH

For the first time in the history of the Black church membership is in decline. Young people are defecting from the church at a rate never seen before. The reason or reasons for this phenomenon escapes even the most insightful analysts. Even the young people who have left the Black church cannot agree as to why this reality is so. Every millennial that has left the church with whom I conducted exit interviews offered a list of reasons for their departures. Most of the reasons seemed to contradict the reasons other millennial interviewees gave for leaving the church. Nevertheless, among the plethora of reasons they provided for their defections, there were some commonalities. They were 1) Disbelief that the Bible is the divinely inspired Word of God. They maintain that the Bible was written by the White man to control the African slaves. 2) Disbelief that Jesus is a historical reality, but he is an invention of the Roman government to be used as a mechanism of control at the whims of the emperor.

3) Belief that the church conspired with the White Male Supremacy System to keep Black people docile and non-resistant to the evils of slavery and oppression. 4) Belief that the church is guilty of duping Black people into accepting their subordinate place in the White Male Supremacy System.

This generation is addicted to the Internet where they are often exposed to misinformation, disinformation and most often, blatant lies. They then share this information with their social media friends who have, also, been influenced by this same misinformation. Social media algorithms group these young people together as a virtual community based upon shared beliefs, interests, and views. Through social media, they reinforce each other's disdain for the church, hardening their opposition to Christianity. Thus, many of them have embraced other religions, and some have even become atheists.

The church's mission is even more difficult than before the *Millennial Defection* began. The church was already challenged to teach and empower its membership to accept the ministry to the "least of these" while simultaneously winning souls to Christ. Now, the church has an additional challenge of reclaiming millennials and their children. I am convinced, however, that if the church is courageous enough to acknowledge this problem and address it in its mission statement, the Holy Spirit will provide the power and resources to solve the problem; whatever the solution may be.

Study Questions

1. Do you think the Internet and social media influence people's decisions to leave the church? Explain.

2. How does the legend of Horus persuade young people to renounce the historicity of Jesus?

3. Why does the White Male Supremacy System want Black people to accept White Jesus?

4. Why does it play into the White Male Supremacy System's agenda when Black people refuse to believe that Jesus ever existed?

5. Why does the White Male Supremacy System celebrate when Black people contend that Jesus' color doesn't matter?

6. Does far right-wing evangelicalism represent the theology, economic, politic, and social agenda Jesus of Nazareth? Explain.

7. What are the differences between how slavery was practiced in the Americas and how it was practiced in biblical Israel?

8. Do you think the Bible supports slavery as it was practiced in the Americas? Explain.

9. Was the Black church complicit in the perpetuation of slavery in the Americas? Explain.

10. Why does Jesus' color matter?

CHAPTER NINE

THE BLESSINGS AND BURDENS OF BLACKNESS

Black people are blessed because theirs is the race through which God revealed God's Self to the world. In the Old Testament, God's Self-revelation came through a Black community called Israel, and in the New Testament, God's Self-revelation was through a Black man named Jesus from Nazareth. After His ascension, God's Self-revelation continued through a group of Black Hebrews who accepted Jesus as Lord and called themselves the People of the Way, the Ecclesia or the Church. The Lord's blessings never come without a burden of responsibility attached. This chapter discusses the obligation of being the Chosen People of God.

Study Guide

1. According to Chapter Nine in *The Bible is Black History*, what are the blessings of blackness? Do you agree with the author? Explain.

2. What is our responsibility as the Chosen People of God? How can we effectively live up to our obligation as God's People?

CHAPTER TEN

A CHALLENGE TO GOD'S CHOSEN PEOPLE

One of the troublesome characteristics of God's people is their stiff-necked stubbornness. God's people have demonstrated this trait too many times throughout biblical and secular history. God's Chosen People have always been easily seduced by surrounding communities to adopt their gods, cultures, traditions, and values; forgetting about their own. Time and again, this behavior provoked God's wrath upon them. Nevertheless, their God remains more than ready to receive them back and shower their community with His blessings. As I have established throughout *The Bible is Black History,* African-Americans are among the descendants of the Lost Tribes of Israel. Beyond all of the historical and DNA evidence, what makes this notion even more compelling is the prophecy in Deuteronomy 28. The curse pronounced on God's people, if they "Refuse to listen to the Lord your God and do not obey..." bears a striking resemblance to the hardships and struggles the African-American community suffers today. The experiences of the African-American community, unlike any other in history, more closely matches the Deuteronomy 28 curse. The good news, however, is that a blessing follows the curse if God's beloved community repents.

Study Guide

1. According to Daniel Lis, one-third of the Africans who were kidnapped from their native land and sold into slavery were Igbos. The majority of African-Americans today are either direct descendants of the Igbos or related by marriage. What does that mean to the African-American community?

2. How does the curse in Deuteronomy 28 apply
    to the African-American community?

3. Do you think it is possible for a community to
    live under a curse for so long that their cursed
    existence seems normal?

4. What must the African-American community do to remove the curse? What is your master strategy to convince the African-American community that its plight is tied to its rebellion against God? How do we persuade our community to repent so that God might restore our fortunes as God's Chosen People as promised in Deuteronomy 28? Share your thoughts on Bibleisblackhistory.com

SUGGESTED READING MATERIALS FOR FURTHER STUDY

The Holy Bible

Alexander, M. (2012). *The New Jim Crow*. New York, NY: New Press

Bonhoeffer, D. (1954). Life Together: *A Discussion of Christian Fellowship*. New York, NY: Harper & Row Publishers

Bruder, E. (2008). *The Black Jews of Africa*. Oxford, UK: Oxford University Press

Cone, J.H. (1975). *God of the Oppressed*. New York, NY: The Seabury Press

Davidson, B. (1969). *The African Genius*. Boston, MA: An Atlantic Monthly Press Book

Dubois, W.E.B. (1903). *The Souls of Black Folks*. New York, NY: Bantam Books

Evans, J. Jr., (1992). *We Have Been Believers*. Minneapolis, MN: Fortress Press

Felder, C. H. (1992). *Troubling Biblical Waters*. Maryknoll, NY: Orbis Books

Hendricks, O. M. Jr. (2006). *The Politics of Jesus*. New York, NY: Doubleday

Ilona, R. (2014). *The Igbos and Israel: An Inter-Cultural Study of the Largest Jewish Diaspora.* Washington, DC: Street to Street EpicCenter Stories

Marble, M. (1983). *How Capitalism Underdeveloped Black America.* Boston, MA: South End Press

McCray, A. (1990). *The Black Presence in the Bible.* Chicago, Ill: Black Light Fellowship

Welsing, F.C. (1991). *The Isis Papers: The Keys To The Colors.* Washington, DC: C.W. Publishing

West, C. (1993). *Race Matters.* Boston, MA: Beacon Press

Williams, R. (1988). *They Stole It But You Must Return It.* Rochester, NY: HEMA Publishing

Windsor, R.R. (1969). *From Babylon to Timbuktu.* Atlanta, GA: Windsor's Golden Series

Woodson, C.G. (1933). *The Mis-education of the Negro.* Trenton, NJ: African World Press

Wright, J. A., Jr. (1995). *Africans who Shaped our Faith.* Chicago, Ill: Urban Ministries, INC

Made in the USA
Coppell, TX
12 April 2024

31209844R10042